The Weeping Time

by Jason Skog

Content Adviser: Stephanie Davenport, Ed.D.,
Director of Education,
DuSable Museum of African-American History

Reading Adviser: Alexa L. Sandmann, Ph.D.,
Associate Professor of Literacy,
Kent State University

Compass Point Books ◆ Minneapolis, Minnesota

Compass Point Books
3109 West 50th Street, #115
Minneapolis, MN 55410

 This book was manufactured with paper containing at least 10 percent post-consumer waste.

On the cover: American Slave Market, 1852 (oil on canvas)

Photographs ©: Chicago History Museum/The Bridgeman Art Library, cover, 26; Prints Old and Rare, back cover (far left); Library of Congress, back cover, 23, 38, 40; North Wind Picture Archives, 5, 16, 25, 28, 36, 39; The Granger Collection, New York, 6, 7, 13, 17, 31, 32, 34; Lee Sneider/Photo Images/Corbis, 8; Courtesy of Hargrett Rare Book and Manuscript Library/University of Georgia Libraries, 10; Brooklyn Museum of Art, New York/The Bridgeman Art Library, 11; Bettmann/Corbis, 12, 18; Print and Picture Collection, The Free Library of Philadelphia, 15; Corbis, 19; Wilberforce House, Hull City Museums and Art Galleries, U.K./The Bridgeman Art Library, 20; Private Collection/The Bridgeman Art Library, 22; Snark/Art Resource, N.Y., 27; Hirshhorn Museum, Washington, D.C./The Bridgeman Art Library, 30; Private Collection/Peter Newark American Pictures/The Bridgeman Art Library, 35.

Editor: Jennifer VanVoorst
Page Production: Ashlee Schultz
Photo Researcher: Svetlana Zhurkin
Cartographer: XNR Productions, Inc.
Library Consultant: Kathleen Baxter

Creative Director: Keith Griffin
Editorial Director: Nick Healy
Managing Editor: Catherine Neitge

Library of Congress Cataloging-in-Publication Data
Skog, Jason.
  The Weeping time / by Jason Skog ; content adviser, Stephanie Davenport ; reading adviser, Alexa L. Sandmann.
      p. cm. — (We the people)
  Includes index.
  ISBN 978-0-7565-3360-1 (library binding)
  1. Slavery—Georgia—Savannah—History—19th century—Juvenile literature. 2. Slave trade—Georgia—Savannah—History—19th century—Juvenile literature. 3. Slaves—Georgia—Savannah—Social conditions—19th century—Juvenile literature. 4. African Americans—Georgia—Savannah—Social conditions—19th century—Juvenile literature. 5. Savannah (Ga.)—History—19th century—Juvenile literature. 6. Savannah (Ga.)—Race relations—History—19th century—Juvenile literature. 7. Butler family—Juvenile literature. 8. Slaveholders—Georgia—Savannah—Biography—Juvenile literature. 9. Savannah (Ga.)—Biography—Juvenile literature. I. Title. II. Series.
  F294.S2S54 2008
  306.3'62089960730758724—dc22   2007035563

Visit Compass Point Books on the Internet at *www.compasspointbooks.com*
or e-mail your request to *custserv@compasspointbooks.com*

TABLE OF CONTENTS

MAJOR BUTLER'S SLAVES

The rain fell for three straight days. The soft ground of the Savannah, Georgia, racetrack was a muddy mess. As the rain fell like tears from the sky, tears streamed like rain from the eyes of many of the hundreds of enslaved people who had been dragged to the Ten Broeck racetrack and sold to the highest bidder. When the two-day auction ended on March 3, 1859, a total of 436 men, women, and children had been sold to new owners.

While babies and the youngest children were allowed to stay with their mothers, most families were torn apart. Older brothers and sisters were separated. Mothers and fathers said goodbye to grown children. Cousins, aunts, and uncles were scattered among various new owners in the southern United States. Even slaves in their teens—considered old enough to work alone on plantations—were ripped from their parents and siblings.

For enslaved families and their descendants, the sale

Families and friends were often separated during slave sales.

became known as The Weeping Time. It was the largest sale of human beings in U.S. history.

The story of the slaves and how they came to be sold at this auction begins with Major Pierce Butler. Born in Ireland and a member of the British army, Butler later fought on the side of the colonies during the Revolutionary War. He helped frame the U.S. Constitution and served as the first U.S. senator from South Carolina. He was

Major Pierce Butler

also a wealthy landowner with two large plantations in Georgia and other property in Philadelphia, Pennsylvania.

All but a handful of the slaves sold at the Savannah racetrack were originally owned by Butler or his descendants. Butler had nearly 1,500 acres (600 hectares) on two plantations in the Georgia Sea Islands. Hundreds of the slaves spent their entire lives toiling in Butler's fields at Hampton Plantation on St. Simons Island and at Butler's Island Plantation on Butler's Island. There they grew cotton and rice and made their owner a very rich man.

The enslaved people who worked on plantations in

An 1859 engraving of a rice planter's mansion in the American South

the Georgia Sea Islands were direct descendants of enslaved Africans brought over from a region of Africa where people were known as skilled farmers, weavers, and cooks. Thus they were considered to be more valuable than many other slaves.

In 1849, a decade before the mass sale, a group of Butler's plantation managers tried to put a value on Butler's property. They counted all of the enslaved people, noting

A chimney is all that remains from a mill on the Butler's Island rice plantation.

their ages and giving the names of family members. Then they put a dollar amount next to each slave's name.

According to the survey, there were 197 family

8

groups—some as small as two members, others as large as 10. What surprised the men who did the study was how long many of the slaves had lived. Of the 840 enslaved people, 55 men and 45 women were 50 years old or older. Renty was the oldest man, at 85. At 75, Evander was the oldest woman. Seven men and seven women were in their 70s.

For decades, the slaves lived and worked together on the Butler land. Many slaves died and were buried on the same plantation where they were born. Having been together so long, many of the enslaved families were related to one another, either by birth or marriage. Even those who were not related had strong friendships and treated one another as though they were family. And like families, they wanted to be together.

THE BUTLER PLANTATIONS

When Major Butler died in 1822, he owned more slaves than almost any other slaveholder in the country and was one of the wealthiest men as well. He left a complicated will that caused his money, property, plantations, and slaves to be divided equally between two of his grandsons, John Butler and Pierce Mease Butler.

Pierce Mease Butler

Pierce Mease Butler was just 12 years old when his grandfather died. In 1826, when he turned 16, he began enjoying his grandfather's enormous wealth, sharing the money with his twin aunts, Frances and Eliza Butler, daughters of Major Butler.

Eager to spend his newfound wealth, Pierce Butler bought new clothes, fine wine, and expensive food. He also gambled and spent his riches on women. One woman in particular caught his eye.

Frances Ann Kemble, known as Fanny, was a popular English actress on a tour of the United States with her father, Charles Kemble. When Butler saw her perform in New York, he instantly fell in love. He followed her for the rest of her U.S. tour, sending her flowers, writing her notes, even performing with the show's musical group just to be near her.

Frances Ann "Fanny" Kemble

11

Fanny Kemble married Pierce Mease Butler in 1834. Though she knew her new husband was wealthy, she did not know how his family had made its money. When she visited the Butler plantations in 1838, she was horrified. She had always opposed slavery, and she was terribly upset by the conditions she saw.

Even before her visit to the South, Fanny Butler and her husband knew that they disagreed on many topics and that perhaps they were not right for each other. Slavery was

Slaves who "misbehaved" were given punishments such as being tied up and soaked with cold water.

the last straw. It was the beginning of the end of a difficult 15-year relationship.

During her nearly two years on Butler's Island Plantation, Fanny wrote in her journal about slave life and how she tried to improve working conditions. In 1863, the journal was published as a book, *Journal of a Residence on a Georgia Plantation*. That was 14 years after her marriage to Pierce Butler had ended and as the country fought the Civil War, with slavery at the center of the conflict.

Pierce Butler's enormous wealth was not enough to keep him out of financial trouble. While his brother John

Enslaved people were often supervised in their work by overseers with whips.

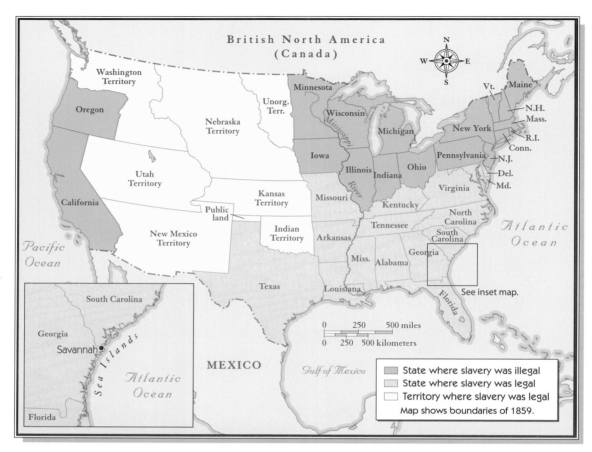

Georgia was one of 15 states that allowed slavery in 1859.

managed his money wisely, Butler spent foolishly.

Butler gambled wildly and invested poorly, losing a lot of money during the nation's financial crisis of 1857–1858. Thirty-seven years after his grandfather's death, he had spent all $700,000 of his inheritance. This would be more than $15 million today. He also owed a great deal of money to creditors.

Control of his estate was transferred to trustees, a group of people responsible for making sure the creditors were paid what they were owed. The trustees quickly sold Butler's fancy Philadelphia home and other property, but it was not enough. Soon they were thinking about selling other "property." It was not long before the enslaved people were heading to the auction block.

Pierce Butler's Philadelphia mansion was sold for $30,000.

DIVIDING THE ESTATE

For many enslaved people, the only thing worse than being a slave was being sold as a slave. Being sold meant they would have a new plantation, a new owner, and new rules—and most likely would be separated from their families and friends.

Slaveholders used the threat of sale and separation from loved ones to force slaves to "behave."

Few of the Butler slaves had been sold before, but that didn't mean it couldn't happen. If an enslaved person was not doing as he or she was told, the threat of being sold was often enough to get the worker to obey.

On the Butler plantations, most of the enslaved people were

farmhands who were good at harvesting rice and cotton. There also were slaves with more specialized skills. There were carpenters who helped maintain the slave quarters and made repairs on the owner's property. There were coopers to make rice buckets, shoemakers to make shoes for the slaves, and blacksmiths to make hoes and other simple tools.

Major Butler had owned more than 900 slaves when he died. Because both grandsons had inherited equal shares

Rice was the primary crop at the plantation on Butler's Island.

Enslaved people cultivated cotton at Hampton Plantation.

of the estate, when it came time to auction the enslaved people, they were divided into two groups of about 450 each. Half belonged to the estate of John Butler, who had died more than 10 years earlier. Those slaves would continue working on the Butler family plantations.

The future of the other slaves, who belonged to Pierce Mease Butler, was less clear. About 20 would continue to live on Butler property. The other 429 men, women, and children were loaded onto railway cars and steamboats and taken to the stables at the Ten Broeck racetrack. Seven slaves from other owners were included in the sale, bringing the total to 436 enslaved people up for auction at the soggy Savannah racetrack.

Word of the auction spread quickly in the weeks preceding the sale. Breaking up such a large family estate was uncommon at the time in the South. Slave owners rarely sold their slaves, so the sale drew many buyers eager to increase their work force. Plantation owners

Some slaves traveled the Savannah River by steamboat on their way to the auction.

from Georgia, South Carolina, North Carolina, Virginia, Alabama, and Louisiana—some traveling hundreds of miles—made their way to Savannah to bid on the slaves. Prospective owners packed every hotel in the city and went to the racetrack in the days before to see the slaves up close.

An 1850s poster advertises a slave auction.

While slave auctions were uncommon and distressing, this was an especially sensitive time for a sale. In 1859, the country was on the verge of a civil war, pitting the Union North against the Confederate South. In the North, abolitionists—those who wanted to ban slavery—were becoming Unionists, people who wanted to keep all the states together.

In the South, those who favored keeping slavery were becoming secessionists. They wanted their states to break free from the rest of the United States and form the Confederate States of America.

An Undercover Reporter

The sale was scheduled for March 2 and 3, 1859. Some of the enslaved people were taken to the racetrack a week before the sale. Until they were led to the auction block, the slaves were kept in the stables. The stables were crowded and smelled of the horses that usually made the wooden pens their home.

An 1850s painting by Eyre Crowe of enslaved people waiting to be auctioned

There were no tables, chairs, or beds. The enslaved people leaned against the walls or rested on their bundles of clothing and other meager belongings. During the rare moments of quiet, they slept on the bare floors.

For meals, they were given rice and beans and the occasional bit of bacon or cornbread. As they waited for the sale, some talked about whether they would be kept together. Others cried quietly. Slave drivers—men with whips and guns who kept the slaves from acting up or running away—watched them night and day.

In the days before the sale, dozens of people

Slave drivers used their whips to threaten slaves.

23

visited the temporary slave quarters to scout out potential purchases. By the time the auction began, more than 200 buyers were in the crowd.

Also in the crowd was Mortimer Neal Thomson, a popular journalist known as "Doesticks." He was the only reporter at the Savannah slave sale. Thomson posed as a plantation owner interested in bidding on some of the slaves that day. He claimed to have $40,000 to spend on slaves—a small fortune at the time. Dressed in his finest clothes, Thomson carried a catalog and a pencil, pretending to make notes on some of the slaves he might be interested in purchasing. In reality, he was writing notes about the auction. His article later appeared in the *New York Tribune* under the headline "What Became of the Slaves on a Georgia Plantation."

Thomson wrote of the enslaved people at the sale, "On the faces of all was an expression of heavy grief; some appeared to be resigned to the hard stroke of Fortune that had torn them from their homes, and were sadly trying to

Slaveholders inspected the enslaved people before the sale.

make the best of it; some sat brooding moodily over their sorrows, their chins resting on their hands, their eyes staring vacantly, and their bodies rocking to and fro, with a restless motion that was never stilled."

While the enslaved people waited anxiously in the

25

An 1852 painting depicts a slave market in the American South.

stables, potential buyers drank in a bar downstairs. As the time for the auction neared, the buyers moved upstairs to a long, narrow room in the grandstand. They lit fresh cigars and flipped open their catalogs, awaiting sight of the first slave.

THE SLAVE AUCTION

Each buyer had been given a catalog before the sale. The catalog listed the name, age, and specialty of each slave. The enslaved people had numbers and descriptions of their conditions. Among them: "116: Rina, Age 18, Rice, Prime Young Woman." And "352: Silas, Age 13, Cotton, Prime Boy."

As the rain fell outside, Pierce Butler walked among the slaves, offering handshakes and goodbyes. The slaves seemed pleased by his presence. The men took off their hats and made a small bow. The women offered a quick curtsy.

A poster advertising an 1856 auction lists slaves and their specialties.

Buyers were less polite in their interactions with the enslaved people. They poked and prodded them, looking for any weakness or injury. They pried open their mouths and inspected their teeth. They pinched their arms and

Buyers examined the slaves' eyes, mouths, and teeth, checking for signs of injury or disease.

legs, checking their muscles. They made them walk up and down a line to see whether they limped. They made them bend over and squat to see whether they were hiding any disability.

All the while, the slaves stayed quiet, unless they hoped to be bought by the person examining them. Although they were supposed to be sold as families, older brothers and sisters often were separated. Eager to stay together, some slaves tried to persuade buyers to take the entire family.

The rain and wind grew worse, blowing through a large opening in the side of the grandstand and delaying the start of the auction by two hours. When the bidding finally began, the slaves looked tired and uncomfortable. The auctioneer, a man by the name of Walsh, stood on a platform at the front of the room and directed the bidding. The first to come forward was a couple named George and Sue, along with their two boys, George and Harry. They were sold as a family for $600 each. The oldest and least-desirable

A 19th-century painting of slaveholders bidding at a slave market

slaves shuffled to the back of the line and watched sadly as the younger ones attracted bids, were sold, and were led off to new owners.

As the rain continued to fall, another family was led to the front for bidding. Primus, a carpenter, was up for sale with his wife, Daphne, and their two young children. Dido was just 3 years old; the other child was just 2 weeks old. Daphne tried to protect her tiny baby from the rain blowing in as they approached the auction block. She covered herself and the infant with a large shawl, but the buyers shouted at the auctioneer, "Pull off her rags!" They asked, "Who's going to bid … if you keep her covered up?" The family sold for $2,500.

More than 30 babies were for sale at the auction. Babies were estimated to be worth about $100 at the time

Enslaved families tried to stay together at the slave auction.

of birth. They increased in value by $100 a year until they were 16 or 17 years old, the age at which they were considered the most valuable.

Along with the anxiety of working for a new owner, slaves worried about being separated from family and

A painting by Thomas Satterwhite Noble of a mother and child at a slave auction

friends. Pierce Butler made it clear to buyers that husbands and wives had to stay together, as well as mothers and very young children. But as reporter Thomson observed, "There is perhaps as much policy as humanity in this arrangement, for thereby many aged and unserviceable people are disposed of, who otherwise would not find a ready sale." Other bonds among slaves, however, were in danger of being broken.

Jeffrey, slave number 319, was 23 years old and unmarried. He sold for $1,310, and he begged his new owner to also buy Dorcas, slave number 278. The two were engaged to be married. Jeffrey was thrilled to hear that the new owner was willing to buy Dorcas as well. But his happiness was short-lived. Dorcas was being sold to another buyer as part of a family of four and could not be bought individually. Jeffrey and Dorcas said goodbye. They never married and never saw each other again.

Another couple, Dembo and Frances, avoided a similar fate. They had hoped to be married before the sale

Enslaved couples who were not married were sold as individuals and usually were forced to part.

but were not. However, they managed to find a minister among those attending that day. They arranged a speedy ceremony and were wed on the spot. They were sold as a pair but were not spared harsh words and cruel jokes from the auctioneer and the crowd.

Some of the enslaved people approached the auction block without showing any emotion. When the winning bid

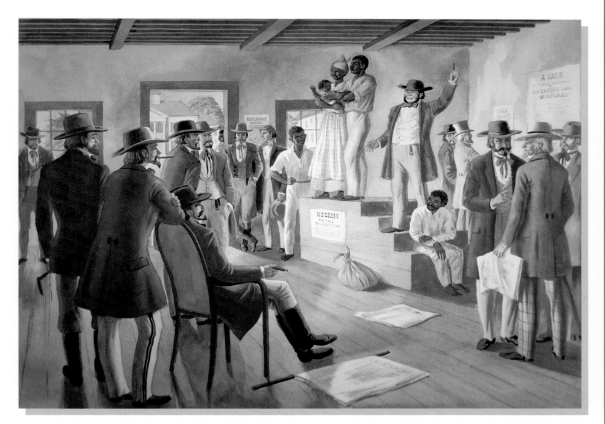

Bidders consider an enslaved family at auction in an 1856 painting.

was announced, they stepped down from the block without even looking at their new owner. Others carefully studied the bidders, watching closely as the bidding narrowed to two. If the owner they favored was winning, they might smile or nod. If the owner they did not want was winning, they frowned, looked away, or wept.

35

AFTER THE SALE

Pierce Butler earned $303,850 from the slave sale. The highest price for one family, a mother and her five grown children, was $6,180. The highest price for a man was $1,750, for William, a "fair carpenter and caulker." The highest price for a woman was $1,250, for Jane, a "cotton hand and house servant." The lowest price was $250 each for Anson and Violet, an older couple in their 50s.

Soon after the last slave was sold, the rain stopped and the sun shone. The fruit trees surrounding

Enslaved people were valued according to the kind and amount of work they could do.

36

the racetrack filled the air with fresh fragrances, and that night the stars sparkled.

Butler visited the slaves before they left and gave each one a dollar—four shiny new quarters—as a thank-you for their service. To the oldest slaves or favorite servants, Butler extended his gloved hand as a farewell.

One of the auction managers sent around baskets filled with bottles of champagne for the owners. Corks popped in celebration. Butler had made enough money to pay his debts and was once again a wealthy man. He left to tour southern Europe before returning home to Philadelphia.

For the slaves sold that day, there was no returning home. Many were forced to say their final goodbyes to their sons and daughters, mothers and fathers, sisters and brothers. None of the enslaved people could read or write, so they could not use letters to stay in touch. Reporter Thomson wrote that "the parents might be left on the old plantation to wear out their weary lives in grief, and lay

A building in Atlanta, Georgia, still had an "Auction & Negro Sales" sign in 1964.

their heads in far-off graves, over which their children might never weep."

In 1863, President Abraham Lincoln issued the Emancipation Proclamation, declaring enslaved people in Confederate territory to be free. Many freed slaves joined the Union Army and fought to preserve the country's unity—and their freedom. In 1865, the bitter Civil War came to an end. That same year, Congress passed the 13th Amendment to the Constitution, banning slavery forever.

After the Civil War, Pierce Butler returned to his family's plantations to try to run them without the help

People in Washington, D.C., gathered to celebrate the abolition of slavery.

of slave labor. But running the plantations was difficult, and the humid climate and wet land invited mosquitoes carrying disease. Butler became ill with malaria and died in 1867.

Some of the Butler family's former slaves also returned to the land they knew best. Some even worked

Once free, some African-Americans returned to the land they had once lived on as slaves.

40

on the same farms, doing the same jobs—this time as sharecroppers. They were free, but they were still far away from the friends and family they once knew.

Of The Weeping Time and its lasting effects, Mortimer Thomson wrote, "The blades of grass on all the Butler estates are outnumbered by the tears that are poured out in agony at the wreck that has been wrought in happy homes, and the crushing grief that has been laid on loving hearts."

GLOSSARY

abolitionists—people who supported the banning of slavery

coopers—barrel makers

creditors—people to whom money or services are owed

estate—the property and possessions left by a person at death

plantations—large farms in the South, usually worked by slaves

secessionists—people who favored slavery and wanted the states that supported slavery to pull out of the Union

sharecroppers—people who work the land in exchange for housing, food, and part of the profits

Unionists—people who supported the North and preserving the union in the Civil War

wrought—created

will—legal document describing who gets what when somebody dies

Did You Know?

- In the War of 1812, British soldiers took 138 slaves from the Butler plantations to Nova Scotia. There the slaves were given the last name "Butler" and set free. Some of the descendants of those slaves still live in Nova Scotia.

- The Weeping Time slave auction was smaller than expected. The earliest advertisements for the auction promised 460 slaves for sale that day. However, some of the oldest slaves were kept back at the Butler plantations and others were sold privately, bringing the final number to 436.

- In a letter to her friend years after The Weeping Time, Fanny Kemble wrote that her former husband, Pierce Butler, had been upset about having to sell his family's slaves. It caused him "extreme pain and mortification," she wrote, though that was not clear by his behavior during the sale.

- Today Interstate 95 crosses the land where the Butler plantations once grew crops of rice, sugar, and cotton. The only former Butler land that is still used as a farm is now owned by a descendant of one of the plantation's former slaves. The rest of the land has become housing developments or wildlife refuges or has been abandoned and allowed to return to wetlands.

IMPORTANT DATES

Timeline

1822	Major Pierce Butler, who owned a large number of slaves, dies; his estate is divided between his grandsons John Butler and Pierce Mease Butler.
1859	Financial losses cause Pierce Mease Butler to sell his portion of the estate's slaves in an auction known as The Weeping Time, held at the Ten Broeck racetrack in Savannah, Georgia.
1861	The American Civil War begins; the conflict pits the North against the South, with slavery at the center of the struggle.
1863	President Abraham Lincoln issues the Emancipation Proclamation, declaring all slaves in Confederate territory free.
1865	The American Civil War ends; Congress passes the 13th Amendment, which bans slavery forever.

IMPORTANT PEOPLE

MAJOR PIERCE BUTLER (1744–1822)

Irish-born soldier, planter, and statesman who was the original owner of the hundreds of slaves sold during The Weeping Time; Butler was also South Carolina's first U.S. senator and is known as one of America's Founding Fathers

PIERCE MEASE BUTLER (1810–1867)

Grandson of Major Pierce Butler, he inherited a fortune but was forced by creditors to sell the slaves in the auction that became known as The Weeping Time

FRANCES ANN "FANNY" KEMBLE (1809–1893)

Famous English actress who married Pierce Mease Butler; they later divorced, disagreeing on the issue of slavery, and she wrote a book about the poor slave conditions at the Butler plantations; in later life, she toured England reading Shakespeare; she also published a volume of poems and several plays

MORTIMER NEAL THOMSON (1831–1875)

Also known as "Doesticks," he was a famous reporter for the New York Tribune *and the only reporter to have witnessed and written about the slave sale*

WANT TO KNOW MORE?

At the Library

Kachur, Matthew. *The Slave Trade.* New York: Chelsea House, 2006.

Lester, Julius. *Day of Tears.* New York: Hyperion Books for Children, 2005.

Lester, Julius. *To Be a Slave.* New York: Dial Books, 1998.

Rossi, Ann. *Freedom Struggle: The Anti-Slavery Movement, 1830–1865.*
   Washington, D.C.: National Geographic, 2005.

On the Web

For more information on this topic, use FactHound.

1. Go to *www.facthound.com*

2. Type in this book ID: 0756533600

3. Click on the *Fetch It* button.

FactHound will find the best Web sites for you.

On the Road

Georgia Historical Society
501 Whitaker St.
Savannah, GA 31401
912/651-2125
Programs and exhibits educate
children and adults on important
aspects of Georgia history

**DuSable Museum of African-
American History**
740 E. 56th Place
Chicago, IL 60637
773/947-0600
Exhibits examine the historical
experiences and achievements of
African-Americans

Look for more We the People books about this era:

The Assassination of Abraham Lincoln
Battle of the Ironclads
The Carpetbaggers
The Confederate Soldier
The Dred Scott Decision
The Emancipation Proclamation
Fort Sumter
The Gettysburg Address
Great Women of the Civil War

The Lincoln-Douglas Debates
The Reconstruction Amendments
Surrender at Appomattox
The Underground Railroad
The Union Soldier
The Weeping Time
Women of the Confederacy
Women of the Union

A complete list of We the People titles is available on our Web site:
www.compasspointbooks.com

INDEX

About the Author

Jason Skog is a writer who lives in Brooklyn, New York, with his wife and son. He has been a newspaper writer for 11 years, covering education, courts, police, government, and youth issues. His work has appeared in *The New York Times,* the *Boston Globe,* the *Baltimore Sun,* magazines, and other newspapers. He is a member of the Society of Children's Book Writers and Illustrators, and this is his fifth book for young readers.